# Unicorns

A
Book
of
Postcards

Pomegranate Artbooks / San Francisco

Pomegranate Communications, Inc.
Box 6099
Rohnert Park, CA 94927
www.pomegranate.com

Pomegranate Europe Ltd.
Fullbridge House, Fullbridge
Maldon, Essex CM9 4LE
England

ISBN 1-56640-959-4
Pomegranate Catalog No. A705

Pomegranate publishes books of
postcards on a wide range of subjects.
Please write to the publisher for more information.

Designed by Mark Koenig

PRINTED IN KOREA

08 07 06 05 04 03 02          13 12 11 10 9 8 7 6 5

To facilitate detachment of the postcards from this book, fold each card along its perforation line before tearing.

The unicorn—a fabulous equine beast, usually pure white, with a single horn growing from the center of its forehead—has been with us, in one form or another, since the dawn of history. First described in China in 2500 B.C. as a miraculous creature called the Ch'i-lin that radiated exquisite colors, had a voice like the tinkling of bells and lived for a thousand years, it has been mentioned in historical accounts in every era and in all parts of the globe, appearing even in the Old Testament. Magical healing and restorative powers have been attributed to its horn—reason enough for any beast with a modicum of common sense to make itself scarce—and doubtless many rhinoceroses, ibexes, narwhals and oxen have perished in the scurrilous trafficking of powdered "unicorn" horn. Gradually the unicorn was given religious significance, becoming associated with purity, divine creativity and spiritual force and symbolizing the presence of the word of God in the Virgin Mary; it played its most prominent role in medieval times, appearing routinely in paintings, tapestries and folklore and continuing to be sighted from time to time, though never allowing itself to be led into captivity.

Through all our attempts to confirm or deny its existence, the unicorn remains a haunting presence stepping delicately through the mists of dream and legend but always slipping just out of view of those who would capture it. Is the unicorn reality or fabrication, a rare, unclassified species or a figment of the imagination? Even if we *could* know once and for all, would we really want to? It may be its very elusiveness that makes the unicorn so appealing: it embodies a spirit of mystery, of magic and undefinable beauty, dwelling forever just beyond our grasp. Perhaps it is enough that a few poets, artists and other visionaries bring us glimpses of it from time to time. Modern-day lovers of the unicorn can take heart: in this collection of postcards, we are pleased to present renditions by five contemporary artists of this timeless, beloved creature.

# Unicorns
Jonathan Meader (American, b. 1943)
*Unicorn II*

Pomegranate, Box 6099, Rohnert Park, CA 94927

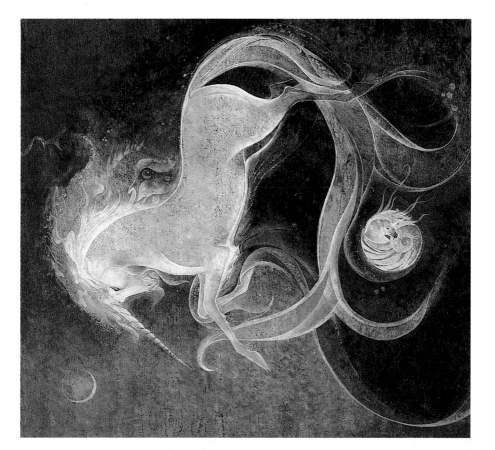

# Unicorns

Susan Seddon Boulet (Brazilian, b. 1941)
*Mystic Unicorn*

Pomegranate, Box 6099, Rohnert Park, CA 94927

# Unicorns

Vaclav Vaca (Czech, b. 1948)
*Unicorns*

Pomegranate, Box 6099, Rohnert Park, CA 94927

# Unicorns
Jay Burch (American)
*Rose Child II*

Pomegranate, Box 6099, Rohnert Park, CA 94927

# Unicorns

Susan Seddon Boulet (Brazilian, b. 1941)
*The Watcher*

Pomegranate, Box 6099, Rohnert Park, CA 94927

# Unicorns
Niki Broyles (American, b. 1947)
*The Mount*

Pomegranate, Box 6099, Rohnert Park, CA 94927

# Unicorns

Vaclav Vaca (Czech, b. 1948)
*Noah's Ark*

Pomegranate, Box 6099, Rohnert Park, CA 94927

# Unicorns
Jay Burch (American)
*Rhinoceros*

Pomegranate, Box 6099, Rohnert Park, CA 94927

# Unicorns
Jonathan Meader (American, b. 1943)
*Dejamour*

Pomegranate, Box 6099, Rohnert Park, CA 94927

# Unicorns

Susan Seddon Boulet (Brazilian, b. 1941)
*Golden Unicorn*

Pomegranate, Box 6099, Rohnert Park, CA 94927

Unicorns
Vaclav Vaca (Czech, b. 1948)
*In Captivity*

Pomegranate, Box 6099, Rohnert Park, CA 94927

# Unicorns
## Jay Burch (American)
*Unicorn of the Fields*

Pomegranate, Box 6099, Rohnert Park, CA 94927

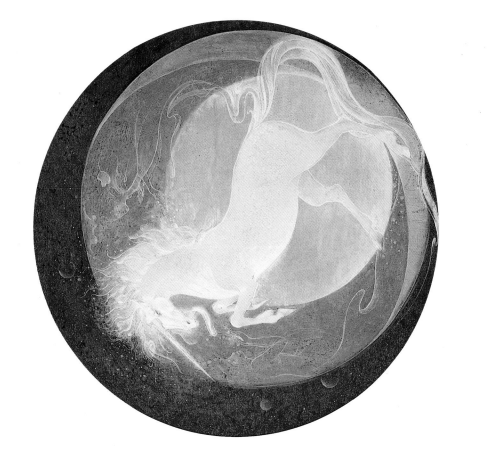

# Unicorns

Susan Seddon Boulet (Brazilian, b. 1941)
*Sovereignty*

Pomegranate, Box 6099, Rohnert Park, CA 94927

# Unicorns

Niki Broyles (American, b. 1947)
*Playtime*

Pomegranate, Box 6099, Rohnert Park, CA 94927

# Unicorns

Vaclav Vaca (Czech, b. 1948)

*The Ship*

Pomegranate, Box 6099, Rohnert Park, CA 94927

# Unicorns

Jay Burch (American)
*The Lyre*

Pomegranate, Box 6099, Rohnert Park, CA 94927

# Unicorns

Susan Seddon Boulet (Brazilian, b. 1941)

*Guardian*

Pomegranate, Box 6099, Rohnert Park, CA 94927

# Unicorns

Niki Broyles (American, b. 1947)
*Bush Stallion*

Pomegranate, Box 6099, Rohnert Park, CA 94927

# Unicorns

Vaclav Vaca (Czech, b. 1948)
*Golden Age*

Pomegranate, Box 6099, Rohnert Park, CA 94927

Unicorns
Jonathan Meader (American, b. 1943)
*Window I*

Pomegranate, Box 6099, Rohnert Park, CA 94927

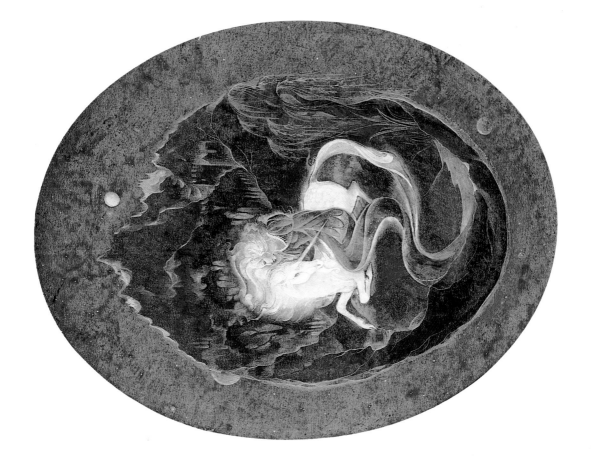

# Unicorns

Susan Seddon Boulet (Brazilian, b. 1941)
*The Unicorn and the Maiden*

Pomegranate, Box 6099, Rohnert Park, CA 94927

Unicorns
Niki Broyles (American, b. 1947)
*The Touch*

Pomegranate, Box 6099, Rohnert Park, CA 94927